The Neuroscience of Stress

Understanding and Overcoming its Effects

Table of Contents

Chapter 1. Introduction

In this Special Report, we delve into the fascinating world of "The Neuroscience of Stress: Understanding and Overcoming its Effects". This is an opportunity to untangle the complex but intriguing web that intertwines our brain, health and stress. Don't worry, no neuroscience degree required! We promise to keep the language simple, clear, and relatable, with practical tips and strategies to empower you. Drawing insights from leading experts, you'll journey into how our brains react to stress, how this affects our physical and mental health, and most importantly, the feasible steps you can take to effectively mitigate stress's impacts. A worthwhile investment into your health and wellbeing, this report is more than just a reading experience; it's the starting point of a more stress-resilient life. Allow us to guide you on this enlightening and enriching adventure. Prepare for new understanding, empowerment and transformation—it all begins here.

Chapter 2. The Science Behind Stress: A Gentle Introduction

Stress is a practically universal experience, woven into the fabric of human life. From the moment we awaken until we close our eyes at night, there are countless potential stressors that impinge upon us. Understanding the science behind stress can illuminate its effects, helping us recognize and address it more effectively.

2.1. Understanding Stress

Stress, at its most basic, can be understood as the body's response to threats or demands, be they physical, mental, or emotional. When we encounter a stressor—a demanding boss, a mountain of bills, a lion on the savannah—our bodies kick into gear, preparing us to confront or evade the threat. This reflex is often referred to as the "fight or flight" response.

In the short term, stress can be beneficial, sharpening our attention and mobilizing energy stores to help us deal with challenges. However, if stress becomes chronic, it can wreak havoc on our health.

Underneath this process lies a complex dance of hormones, orchestrated by the brain. The hypothalamus, a small region at the base of the brain, is the conductor of this hormonal opera, triggering a cascade of hormones from the adrenal glands, including cortisol and adrenaline. These hormones flood our system, raising heart rate, blood pressure, and glucose levels, arming us with the energy and focus needed to meet the stressor head on.

2.2. The Connection Between Stress and the Brain

Stress doesn't just originate in the brain—it affects the brain, too. Chronic stress has been linked to a litany of mental health issues, ranging from anxiety and depression to memory problems and decreases in cognitive function.

Research has revealed that chronic stress can actually shrink certain parts of the brain, including the prefrontal cortex, which is responsible for higher cognitive functions like decision making and social behavior, and the hippocampus, which plays a key role in memory formation.

On the other hand, it can increase the size of the amygdala, the brain's fear center. This not only makes us more sensitive to stress—it also primes the brain to respond more aggressively to future stressors.

2.3. The Physical Implications of Stress

As powerful as its effects can be on mental health, stress's reach extends to the physical body as well. For instance, stress has been linked to a higher risk of certain chronic illnesses, including heart disease, hypertension, diabetes, and obesity.

During periods of stress, your body is in a continual "fight or flight" mode. Continuous release of stress hormones can lead to increased inflammation, which over time can trigger a series of health issues, from simpler problems such as headaches and sleep disorders to more severe issues like cardiovascular disease.

2.4. Stress Perception and Personalized Stress Response

Just as stress affects everyone, everyone also perceives and responds to stress in their own unique way. Some thrive under pressure, while others go to pieces. Some seek out stressful situations, while others avoid them like the plague. This variability has roots in our genetics, upbringing, and environment.

Genetically, some people may be predisposed to react more strongly to stress. They may have a heightened stress response due to variations in genes that regulate serotonin, a mood-influencing neurotransmitter, or the cortisol response.

Environmental factors play a substantial role as well—someone who grew up in a volatile home may have a heightened stress response, even as an adult. In contrast, someone who enjoyed a stable, supportive upbringing may be better equipped to manage stress.

2.5. Coping with Stress: An Integrative Approach

Understanding stress means more than just understanding its causes and effects—it also means understanding how to deal with it. For all its potential harm, stress isn't inherently bad. It's how we respond to it that determines its impact.

One of the most effective ways to cope with stress is through what psychologist and stress researcher Richard Lazarus termed "cognitive appraisal." This involves reframing the ways we look at stressors and our capacity to cope.

Mind/Body practices, such as meditation, yoga, and other relaxation techniques, can also be very effective in combating stress. These practices help foster a sense of calm and balance, buffering the effects of stress.

Additionally, physical activity is a potent stress-buster. Exercise helps to dilute stress hormone levels and stimulates production of feel-good endorphins.

A balanced diet rich in fruits, vegetables, lean proteins, healthy fats and whole grains can also help buffer the body against the effects of stress. Certain foods are known to be particularly beneficial in managing stress, including those rich in vitamin C, omega-3 fatty acids, and magnesium.

In developing a comprehensive stress management approach, it's critical to tailor it to individual needs and preferences. There's no one-size-fits-all answer to stress—we're all different and what works for one person may not work for another.

Understanding the science behind stress can help illuminate the path to a healthier, less stressful life. By recognizing its triggers and effects, individuals can gain a finer control over their reactions to stress, devising coping strategies that cater to their unique needs. It's clear that stress doesn't have to be overwhelming—it can actually be an opportunity for personal growth and resilience. Let's embrace the challenge and learn how to thrive, despite the stressors in our lives.

Chapter 3. Breaking Down the Brain: Understanding Its Role in Stress

To understand the role the brain plays in stress, it's essential to delve into the structure and functionality of our central command center. The human brain, an organ as mystifying as it is crucial, operates to regulate virtually all human activity, including our response to stress.

3.1. The Brain's Anatomy

The brain is a complex entity, made up of approximately 100 billion neurons. It's divided into several different sections, each playing a unique role in stress response.

The primary structures we'll focus on are the amygdala, hypothalamus, pituitary gland, and the adrenal (HPA) axis. These different areas coordinate to manage our brain's response to stress.

The amygdala, one of the key players, triggers the initial stress response. This almond-shaped cluster in our brain processes emotions, such as fear and anxiety. When we encounter a stressful situation, the amygdala sends an alert to the hypothalamus, which is often described as our brain's command center.

The hypothalamus, responsible for many bodily functions, from hunger to sleep to body temperature, receives this stress signal and jumps into action. It commences communication with the rest of the body through the nervous system, utilizing a specific division called the Autonomic Nervous System (ANS).

The ANS, split into the parasympathetic and sympathetic nervous systems, manages our body's immediate and longer-term stress responses. The sympathetic system triggers "fight or flight" mode, initiating a series of rapid physiological changes. Conversely, the parasympathetic system promotes "rest and digest," aiming to bring the body back to stability when the perceived threat is over.

When the hypothalamus activates the sympathetic nervous system, it also sparks the `hypothalamus-pituitary-adrenal (HPA) axis`. This intricate network begins with the hypothalamus, which releases corticotropin-releasing hormone (CRH). This hormone promotes the release of the adrenocorticotropic hormone (ACTH) from the pituitary gland, ultimately leading to cortisol production in the adrenal glands.

3.2. The Stress Response: From Perception to Reaction

Stress begins as a psychological perception. When we encounter a stressor - whether it's physical, such as a lion charging towards us, or psychological, like a demanding work deadline - our amygdala sets the stress response process in motion.

This kicks off the cascade we walked through earlier: The amygdala alerts the hypothalamus > hypothalamus triggers the ANS and HPA axis > these systems work together to prepare the body to deal with the perceived threat.

In the "fight or flight" phase, various physiological changes occur — the heart rate speeds up, blood pressure rises, and adrenaline and cortisol levels increase. These changes mobilize energy stores and enhance focus, preparing us to either confront the danger or make a quick getaway.

But not all stress results in such dramatic physical responses. In the case of chronic stress or ongoing emotional stress, the HPA axis sustains a state of prolonged cortisol release. Prolonged exposure to elevated cortisol can have deleterious effects on the body, leading to a host of health issues ranging from depression and anxiety to high blood pressure and heart disease.

3.3. Impact of Chronic Stress on the Brain

While acute, or short-term, stress can be beneficial for survival, chronic stress can damage the brain in several ways.

First, chronic stress can lead to changes in brain structure and function. Elevated cortisol levels can affect various brain regions, leading to alterations in the volume of certain areas, like the prefrontal cortex and hippocampus.

Second, continuous stress can cause neurochemical changes, affecting neurotransmitters such as serotonin and dopamine, which play a vital role in mood regulation.

Third, chronic stress can hamper neurogenesis, the creation of new neurons, particularly in the hippocampus. This can impair memory and make it harder to manage stress in the future.

Finally, chronic stress can lead to neuronal death, where sustained high cortisol levels can kill brain cells, particularly in the hippocampus.

3.4. Building Stress Resilience: Protecting the Brain

Now, the big question is, how can we protect our brains from the effects of chronic stress? There are several strategies, such as:

1. Regular exercise: Physical activity has been shown to reduce cortisol levels, improve mood, and even promote neurogenesis.

2. Mindfulness and meditation: These techniques lower stress levels and enhance our capacity to manage stress, by changing the way our brains respond to stressors.

3. Adequate sleep: Proper and regular sleep helps to regulate the systems that manage stress response in our brains.

4. Nutritious diet: Certain nutrients can support brain health and resilience to stress, such as Omega-3 fatty acids, B vitamins, and antioxidants.

5. Social connections: Cultivating positive relationships can lower stress levels and provide emotional resources to cope with stressors.

In conclusion, understanding the role of the brain in stress helps us find ways to manage stress more effectively. By supporting our brain and its functions, we can build resilience to stress and lead healthier, happier lives.

Chapter 4. Chemistry of Stress: Harmful or Helpful?

Our brains, in their most basic operational mode, are designed to keep us safe. To achieve this, they constantly monitor our surroundings for potential threats. It's the autonomic nervous system, particularly the sympathetic nervous system, that's responsible for our body's rapid involuntary response to dangerous or stressful situations. When faced with a situation perceived as a threat, our brains trigger a swift release of hormones that prepare our bodies for what's widely known as the 'fight or flight' response.

4.1. An Overview of Stress Chemistry

To dive in, let's first decipher the players involved. The 'stress hormones' we often hear about are primarily cortisol, adrenaline, and norepinephrine. When a stressful situation is detected, the hypothalamus, a small region at the base of our brain, stimulates the adrenal glands to release these hormones.

Adrenaline, also known as epinephrine, boosts our heart rate, blood pressure, and energy supplies. Cortisol, meanwhile, suppresses non-emergency bodily functions like our immune response and digestion, curbs functions that could be detrimental in a fight or flight situation, and enhances the body's ability to use glucose and the brain's use of glucose while also maintaining the availability of substances that repair tissues. Moreover, cortisol prevents the release of substances in the body that cause inflammation.

While this hormonal surge is intended for short-term bursts of energy—enough to outmaneuver danger—chronic exposure due to long-term stress can be detrimental, leading us to our next discussion.

4.2. Chronic Stress and Its Implications

When we are continually exposed to stressors, the constant rush of these hormones can lead to a variety of health problems. Chronic stress disrupts nearly every system in your body. These disruptions can lead to a myriad of problems, such as:

1. 1) Impaired cognitive performance
2. 2) Suppressed thyroid function
3. 3) Blood sugar imbalances
4. 4) Decreased bone density
5. 5) Lowered immunity and inflammatory responses
6. 6) Increased blood pressure
7. 7) Increased abdominal fat, which has a stronger correlation with certain health problems than fat deposited in other areas of the body.

The link between chronic stress and heart disease is particularly alarming, given the profound effects of stress hormones on heart rate and blood pressure. Moreover, overexposure to cortisol may lead to osteoporosis, arthritis, and other conditions due to prolonged suppression of bone formation and immune response.

4.3. The Positive Role of Stress: Eustress

In contrast to what we've looked at, not all stress is bad for our bodies. In certain circumstances, stress plays a crucial role in motivating us to act, helping us concentrate, work hard, and react quickly. Known as 'eustress', which stands for 'good stress', this type of stress has been associated with life satisfaction and well-being.

Eustress, akin to its negative counterpart - 'distress', triggers a surge of adrenaline and norepinephrine. However, the stressors in this situation are usually situations that are perceived as manageable or even exciting. The biochemical changes that eustress triggers can deliver an exhilarating thrill, helping improve performance on challenging but enjoyable tasks. An uptick in heart rate, faster brainwaves, and heightened senses can be invigorating when it's in response to an anticipated positive challenge.

4.4. Strategies to Manage Stress: Hormones

In the face of chronic stress, altering the body's biochemical response becomes vital. One proven method to reduce the quantity of stress hormones in the body is through regular physical activity. Exercise reduces cortisol levels and stimulates endorphin production, the body's natural mood elevators.

Other strategies that can assist in chemical stress management include adequate rest, proper nutrition, and mindfulness-based practices such as meditation and yoga. These practices help to lower cortisol levels, balance blood glucose, and increase resilience in the face of stress.

Moreover, building supportive relationships and social networks can provide emotional assistance, helping tamp down the body's production of stress hormones.

4.5. Biomarkers of Stress: Monitoring Your Body's Response to Stress

Lastly, it can be beneficial to understand how your body responds to stress. Biomarkers such as cortisol levels in your saliva or the presence of certain antibodies in your blood can indicate your body's stress exposure and your physiological resilience. With this knowledge, you can develop a personalized strategy for managing stress and its biochemical impacts.

In summary, stress, a ubiquitous part of life, triggers a chain of chemical reactions in our body. While the acute stress response prepares us for immediate challenges, long-term chronic stress can lead to a host of health problems by continuously flooding our system with stress hormones. Conversely, positive stress, or eustress, can energize and strengthen our bodies and minds. Understanding how our bodies respond to stress at a biochemical level is the first step towards channelling and handling it healthily. Armed with this knowledge, you equip yourself to create a more balanced, resilient life.

Chapter 5. Stress and Your Health: Unraveling the Connection

Stress is a word frequently thrown around in daily conversations. A high-pressure job, multifarious home responsibilities, or even traffic can trigger our stress response. Did you know, however, that stress's relationship with our health runs much deeper than merely causing us to feel 'stressed out'? To begin this journey, we'll first decode the enigma of stress and its fundamental relationship with our health.

5.1. Understanding Stress

Stress is a natural response with deep evolutionary roots. Our ancestors experienced stress as an essential survival mechanism, better known as the 'fight or flight' response. This response geared them up to either confront a threat (fight) or flee (flight) during dangerous situations, such as a predator's attack. It involved an acute physiological reaction where the body flooded with adrenaline, cortisol, and other hormones to prepare the individual to react rapidly and appropriately to the threat.

In today's world, we no longer face these primal threats, yet our body's reaction to stress remains virtually the same. This response, useful for our ancestors, isn't always ideal in our current environment. The sources of stress today "ongoing pressures and worries from work, family responsibilities, and other aspects of everyday life " can trigger this reaction frequently. This regular activation of our stress response can place an enormous strain on our bodies, leading to a slew of health problems if left unchecked.

5.2. The Neurological Underpinnings of Stress

To get a firm grasp of stress and its health impact, we need to delve into our body's control center - the brain. During stressful events, our brain's hypothalamic-pituitary-adrenal (HPA) axis becomes activated. Starting with the hypothalamus, it releases corticotropin-releasing hormone (CRH), which then signals the pituitary gland to release adrenocorticotropic hormone (ACTH). ACTH travels through the bloodstream to the adrenal glands, telling them to release cortisol, our primary stress hormone.

Cortisol, in the short term, is beneficial. It allows us to remain focused, regulates metabolism, reduces inflammation, and provides the energy needed to manage stressful situations. However, if our stress response is frequently activated, leading to higher cortisol levels persistently, it can wreak havoc on our bodies in the long run.

Increased cortisol over time can suppress the immune system, increase blood pressure, contribute to weight gain, impair memory and learning, and even diminish bone density, to name a few. This discussion brings us to the next critical part of our journey - how stress impacts our health.

5.3. The Impact of Stress on Physical Health

There is a strong nexus between long-term exposure to stress and a host of physical health conditions. Let's look at some of these in detail:

Cardiovascular Disease: Stress can directly increase heart rate and blood flow, causing the release of cholesterol and triglycerides into the bloodstream. Over time, these physiological changes can lead to hypertension, heart disease, or even a stroke.

Weight Problems: Stress impacts our metabolism and eating habits, leading to weight gain, obesity, and related issues. Prolonged exposure to cortisol can lead to an increase in appetite, which makes us reach for comfort, usually unhealthy, food.

Digestive Issues: Stress can affect digestion, leading either to constipation or diarrhea. Over the long term, it can result in more severe gastrointestinal issues like irritable bowel syndrome (IBS), gastritis, and acid reflux disease.

Immune System Dysfunction: Chronic stress weakens our immune system, making us more susceptible to infections, prolonging the healing process, and even exacerbating allergies.

Other Conditions: Chronic stress is also linked to numerous other conditions such as insomnia, skin conditions like acne or eczema, and menstrual problems in women.

5.4. Stress and Mental Health: Two Sides of the Same Coin?

Stress doesn't stop at harming our physical wellness; it can heavily impact our mental health too. When perceived threats trigger our stress response, the increased cortisol can cause us to feel anxiety, irritability, or depression. These signs can manifest as withdrawal from social situations, decreased productivity at work, or a general feeling of being overwhelmed.

Research has also demonstrated a strong connection between chronic psychological stress and mental health disorders. Excessive, long-term stress can increase the risk of depression, anxiety disorders, and even post-traumatic stress disorder (PTSD).

5.5. Overcoming the Effects of Stress: Practical Steps

Understanding the link between stress and health underscores the need to manage stress effectively. Here are a few practical steps everyone can integrate into their lifestyle:

Mindfulness and Meditation: Regularly practicing mindfulness and meditation can lower stress levels, counterbalancing its harmful effects.

Exercise Regularly: Physical activity not only improves your mood but can also act as a natural stress antidote. Find an activity you enjoy and make it a part of your routine.

Balanced Diet: Eating a balanced diet can help manage weight and provide essential nutrients that protect the body against the effects of stress.

Ample Sleep: Getting enough sleep is essential to recover from stressful events and prepare for new challenges.

Connect with Others: Social support plays a crucial role in stress management. Reach out to friends and family, talk about your feelings, and never hesitate to seek professional help if needed.

Avoid Unhealthy Habits: Some of us resort to coping mechanisms like drinking, smoking, or overeating. While they may offer temporary relief, these habits can exacerbate health problems in the long run.

Relaxation Techniques: Techniques like progressive muscle relaxation, deep breathing, and yoga can help reduce stress levels and improve well-being.

Bask in Nature: Spending time outdoors has been shown to reduce stress and improve overall well-being.

Through informed efforts and supportive strategies, stress can become a manageable part of life, rather than a paralyzing force. As we move forward, it's crucial to remember that it's okay to ask for help and acknowledge that stress affects us. Our health doesn't have to be a casualty of stress; in fact, by correctly understanding and managing stress, we can cultivate resilience and healthfulness that can last a lifetime.

Chapter 6. Stress Indicators: Reading Your Body's Signals

Every individual responds to stress in different ways, but there are commonalities underlying these reactions. Both our brains and bodies communicate signs of stress, and getting to understand these signals can be the first crucial step in managing stress effectively. Let's explore them further.

6.1. Physical Indicators of Stress

Physical manifestations of stress can often be subtle, coming on gradually, and can be easily overlooked or dismissed as unrelated to stress, hence the need to pay careful attention to changing patterns of physical wellbeing. Here are some commonly experienced physical symptoms:

1. Sleep Disruptions: Stress can lead to difficulties in falling asleep, staying asleep, experiencing non-refreshive sleep, or even, paradoxically, excessive sleepiness.

2. Changes in Appetite: Noticeable shifts in eating habits and weight, whether it's eating more or less than usual.

3. Muscle Tension: Tense, tight muscles or unexplained aches and pains are common under stress.

4. Digestive Problems: Stress impacts gut health and can result in symptoms like constipation, diarrhea, or other digestion-related discomfort.

5. Fatigue: Feeling excessively tired or drained, regardless of sleep quality, could be a sign of stress.

6. Headaches: Stress headaches, or "tension" headaches, manifest as discomfort or pressure in the forehead or the back of the head.

Being mindful of any changes in your physical state can help you acknowledge possible stress conditions. Linking symptoms with phases of increased stress or challenging events is a good way to recognize possible stressors.

6.2. Emotional Indicators of Stress

Stress can significantly influence our emotional state, which can be even more challenging to recognize than physical signs. These emotional changes often seep into various aspects of daily life, impacting personal relationships and professional performance. Here are some common emotional signs:

1. Mood Swings: Unpredictable shifts in your mood, including irritability, anger, or sadness.

2. Anxiety: High stress levels can trigger feelings of unease, worry, or fear.

3. Difficulty in Relaxing: An inability to calm down, constantly feeling on edge or nervous.

4. Feeling Overwhelmed: A sense of dread, or that difficulties are piling up faster than you can manage them.

5. Lack of Motivation: Diminished interest in pursuits you ordinarily enjoy, or a general lack of enthusiasm.

6. Low Self-esteem: Stress can sow seeds of self-doubt and lead to feelings of worthlessness.

Emotional signs of stress can be much more intrusive than physical ones, but recognizing these signs requires deep introspection and self-awareness. An emotional self-check can keep your mental wellbeing in check.

6.3. Cognitive Indicators of Stress

Stress can also impact cognitive functions, affecting processes like memory, attention, and decision making. You may experience:

1. Memory Problems: Trouble recalling events, forgetfulness, or "brain fog".

2. Difficulty Concentrating: Struggling to stay focused on one task at a time or easily getting distracted.

3. Poor Judgment: Making quick decisions without considering the outcomes or difficulty making decisions.

4. Persistent Worrying: Stress can often put us into a cycle of endless worry and negative thinking.

Identifying cognitive symptoms of stress can encourage you to take stress management strategies into closer consideration. Cognition is crucial for the successful execution of daily activities, and impairments in this can be a significant red flag.

6.4. Behavioral Indicators of Stress

Behavioral changes may also reflect increased stress levels. You might notice:

1. Changes in Sleep and Eating Habits: As mentioned earlier under physical signs, stress can significantly impact these routines.

2. Procrastination: Delay or avoidance in carrying out tasks that require immediate attention.

3. Nervous Behaviors: Fidgeting, pacing, biting nails, or other restless activities can signal stress.

4. Substance Use: Increased reliance on substances like alcohol, caffeine, nicotine, or other drugs to cope.

Observing changes in your own behaviours or getting feedback from loved ones might help identify these changes sooner.

Acknowledge these stress signals your body sends you. Responding to these signs early on can make a significant difference in managing stress before it spirals out of control. Stress management strategies, including mindfulness techniques, physical activity, good nutrition, sufficient sleep, and professional help when necessary, can contribute to the effective management of stress.

Remember, stress is not merely a state of mind or an inevitable part of life. It manifests physically, emotionally, cognitively, and behaviorally, and, left unmanaged, can lead to long-term deterioration of health and wellbeing. Thus, decoding and attending to these stress signals promptly is crucial in pursuing a healthy, fulfilling life.

Understanding stress is a step towards empowerment. Only when we acknowledge it can we begin to take control of it. So, listen to your body, take note of its signals, and take the necessary steps to foster resilience. Despite stress being a ubiquitous aspect of modern life, you have the power to overcome it. Embark on the journey of stress mastery and take charge of your well-being.

Chapter 7. Mental Health Under Siege: Exploring Stress's Psychological Impacts

Stress has been a relentless companion of humanity throughout its evolution—its undoubted value lies in how it has primed us for the life-or-death situations our ancestors regularly faced. However, its role and effects in our current societal context, with its myriad pressures, prompt a highly pertinent discourse.

7.1. The Brain on Stress

Before we delve into how stress impacts our mental health, let's understand our brain's response to stress on a fundamental level. The brain acts as a central command station, processing information, signals, pressure, and potential threats. When a stressor—whether it's an imminent physical threat or perceived emotional pressure— is identified, your brain triggers the release of hormones such as adrenaline and cortisol.

Adrenaline heightens your senses, increases heart rate, and prepares your 'flight or fight' response. Cortisol, on the other hand, is responsible for maintaining fluid balance and blood pressure while suppressing the body's immune response. It also reduces non-emergency bodily functions, like the digestive and reproductive systems, and suppresses growth processes. This orchestration is all behind the survival-focused state of high alert.

But what happens when this state prolongs or when the brain misinterprets stressors?

7.2. Chronic Stress: The New Normal

Today, for many people, the brain's 'fight or flight' response is being activated far too often, and the body doesn't always have a chance to return to normal, resulting in what we call chronic stress. This situation is akin to having your car's engine running all the time. Over time, chronic stress can lead to significant mental health problems.

Chronic stress increases the risk of developing psychiatric disorders like depression and anxiety, worsens symptoms of existing mental illnesses, and can lead to cognitive issues like memory loss and concentration impairment. Let's explore these interplays further.

7.3. Stress and Depression

Chronic stress is a significant risk factor for developing depression. Sustained high levels of cortisol can reduce levels of serotonin and dopamine—two 'feel-good' chemicals in the brain—which can trigger symptoms of depression.

Overstressed individuals may also find themselves trapped in a cycle of negative thinking, as chronic stress can foster maladaptive cognitive processes such as rumination and catastrophizing. This pattern sets the stage for depressive thoughts and feelings to thrive.

7.4. Stress and Anxiety Disorders

More often than not, stress and anxiety are two sides of the same coin. Chronic stress may increase your risk of developing anxiety disorders. Your 'fight or flight' response can go into overdrive, affecting your peace of mind and quality of life. Symptoms can range from constant worry and tension to panic attacks. Chronic stress can also exacerbate symptoms of pre-existing anxiety disorders.

7.5. Cognitive Implications of Chronic Stress

High stress levels can impair cognitive functions such as attention, perception, learning, and memory. This feedback loop can further increase stress, leading to a downward mental spiral. Persistently high stress levels can trigger the generation of stress proteins that may cause structural changes in the brain, potentially contributing to chronic cognitive impairment.

Another concern is the impact on the hippocampus—a brain region critical for learning and memory—which is particularly sensitive to chronic stress. Sustained cortisol release may shrink the hippocampus, impairing memory abilities and elevating the risk of certain dementias.

7.6. The Vulnerable Youth

An alarming trend is the escalating stress levels among children and young adults. Exposure to high levels of stress at an early age can trigger mental health conditions. Stress-coping mechanisms aren't fully developed in the younger population, making them more vulnerable to toxic stress experiences. This early-onset stress can lead to a higher risk of developing mental health disorders later in life.

7.7. Buffering the Siege: Building Resilience

While the impacts of stress on mental health can be severe, they're not unavoidable. By building resilience—the ability to cope with and bounce back from adverse situations—we can effectively buffer the mental siege of stress.

Cultivating resilience isn't solely about having the strength to endure stressful times but more about learning to draw upon the skills and support needed to navigate the storm efficiently. This resilience can be built through a combination of personal coping strategies, social support networks, and professional help.

Personal coping strategies involve mindful practices such as meditation, yoga, and relaxation exercises, along with maintaining a healthy lifestyle through adequate sleep, balanced diet, and regular exercise. A robust social support network of friends, family, and community can provide emotional sustenance during stressful times.

Mental health professionals can guide you through cognitive-behavioral therapy or other therapeutic practices aimed at changing the patterns of thinking or behavior behind your stress. They can arm you with the skills to tackle stress and reduce its mental health impact.

Our potential to effectively mitigate the psychological impacts of stress is promisingly high. A stress-resilient life is achievable through persistent efforts to understand stress patterns, proactive lifestyle changes, and willingness to seek professional help.

Isn't it time we stopped letting stress hold our mental health captive? We have the power to counteract stress, buffering its siege on our mental health. Armed with this knowledge, let's act to transform our understanding into empowerment. It's not just about surviving stress—it's about thriving despite it.

Chapter 8. Crossing Ages and Cultures: Stress in Different Demographics

If we sift through the sands of history or traverse the expanses of the modern world, one thread that ties all human experiences together is stress. It's an universal phenomenon, but it's also a chameleon, changing its colors depending on a host of variables.

Despite its ubiquity, the stress experienced by an individual can differ greatly based on numerous factors, including age, gender, culture, and living conditions. Let's probe further into this intriguing relationship.

8.1. Understanding Stress across Ages

Let's begin our voyage by exploring the different forms of stress across age groups.

In infants and toddlers, stress often arises from physical discomfort or separation from caregivers. As they can't communicate their feelings adequately, they often express stress through crying or physical cues like restlessness and disrupted sleep. Research suggests that prolonged exposure to stress in early life can lead to developmental delays and may predispose children to mental health disorders later in life.

As children grow into adolescence, academic pressures, peer relationships, and hormonal changes pile stress onto their developing brains. They're also navigating an increasingly complex socio-emotional landscape, often leading to new stressors. The

American Psychological Association reported that nearly 30% of teenagers are feeling overwhelmed due to stress and 40% reported feeling irritable or angry.

For adults, the pressures of balancing work, family and social commitments can create an environment ripe for stress development. Financial worries and health issues also frequently contribute. In old age, physical health declines, loved ones may pass away, and feelings of loneliness can increase stress levels, affecting both physical and mental wellbeing.

8.2. Gender and Stress

Stress is not gender-blind. In fact, significant differences between the genders straight down to their neurobiological responses to stress have been observed.

Statistically, women report higher stress levels when compared to their male counterparts. They are more likely to experience physical symptoms of stress like headache, upset stomach, and are more prone to psychological issues like depression or anxiety. Hormonal fluctuations, societal pressures and biological differences contribute to these gender variances in stress.

On the other hand, men, faced with stress, are more likely to develop issues like heart disease, hypertension, and diabetes. These disparities reiterate the importance of gender-sensitive approaches in managing stress.

8.3. Culture and Stress

Cultural contexts also shape our perception and experience of stress significantly.

Different cultures have different attitudes towards expression of stress and mental health. In many Eastern cultures, there might be a tendency to suppress stress or anxiety, often due to societal stigma associated with mental health. In contrast, Western cultures usually encourage acknowledging mental stress.

Culture can also influence coping mechanisms. While more individualistic societies might promote tackling problems head on, in collectivist cultures, people may prefer seeking social support when under stress.

8.4. Living Conditions and Stress

Socioeconomic factors and living conditions are strong stress determinants. Poverty, food insecurity, and lack of access to healthcare are significant stress drivers among the economically disadvantaged. On the flipside, those in thriving conditions might experience stress from work overload, societal expectations, or maintaining their status.

Across ages, genders, cultures, or living conditions, stress proves to be an intricate issue with diverse manifestations. Untangling these strands is crucial to holistically understand stress and devise appropriate stress management strategies.

8.5. Strategies for Mitigating Stress

Ultimately, our goal is not merely to understand stress in all its complexity, but to equip ourselves with the tools to cope with it effectively. Our coping strategies need to be just as diverse and tailored as the stressors themselves.

- Mindfulness and meditation introduce calmness into our lives, with numerous studies demonstrating their benefits across demographics.
- Regular physical activity is an excellent way to reduce stress,

improve mood, and enhance overall wellbeing.

- A balanced diet can fuel the body and mind, helping us better cope with day-to-day stressors.

- Maintaining strong social networks is crucial. Whether it's a chat with a loved one or seeking professional help, don't underestimate the power of a good conversation.

- For children and teens, parents and teachers can play vital roles in identifying signs of stress and providing emotional support.

- In tackling stress related to living conditions or socioeconomic factors, broader discussions on systemic changes and social justice are necessary.

This look at stress across the dimensions of age, gender, culture and living conditions paints a rich and complex picture. Undeniably, stress is a dynamic, multifaceted phenomenon that needs to be viewed through diverse lenses. Armed with this understanding, we are better prepared for actionable change—to foster stress resilience and enhance overall wellness.

Chapter 9. Stress Management Techniques: Science-Backed Strategies

In today's fast-paced world, stress is an undeniable fact of life. Equally undeniable is the compelling body of scientific evidence showcasing the effectiveness of certain stress management techniques. We're here to break down those practices, their underlying neuroscience, and how you can implement them in your life.

9.1. Understanding Stress

Before we start with the techniques, it's crucial to comprehend what we're dealing with. So, what exactly is stress? Whenever we face an event or situation that threatens our wellbeing, our brain responds by activating a system known as the "fight-or-flight" response. The adrenal glands release two hormones—adrenaline and cortisol—that prepare our body to either fight the threat or run from it. However, prolonged exposure to these hormones due to constant stressors can wreak havoc on our physical and mental health.

Now that we've discussed what stress is, let's delve into some proven techniques for managing it.

9.2. Deep Breathing

Arguably the most fundamental, deep breathing initiates the relaxation response, counteracting the body's fight-or-flight response. Research has shown that deep breathing can reduce cortisol levels, thereby reducing symptoms of stress.

Here's a simple deep breathing technique you can practice:

1. Sit comfortably, closing your eyes and taking a few normal breaths.

2. Take a slow, deep breath, filling your lungs as much as possible.

3. Hold your breath for a brief moment.

4. Then exhale slowly, allowing all the air to flow out of your chest.

5. Repeat this cycle for a few minutes or until you feel calmer.

9.3. Progressive Muscle Relaxation

Another technique grounded in science is Progressive Muscle Relaxation (PMR). Studies hint that PMR can minimize stress symptoms and improve sleep quality. The principle is simple: tense and then relax each muscle group in your body. As you relax, you'll start feeling a sense of deep relaxation.

PMR procedure:

1. Begin by finding a quiet place and making yourself comfortable.

2. Start with your toes. Tense them for about five seconds and then relax for 30 seconds. Repeat the cycle before moving to the next muscle group.

3. Gradually work your way up to your lower legs, thighs, stomach, back, arms, hands, neck, and finally, your face.

4. Practice this regularly for optimal benefits.

9.4. Mindfulness Meditation

Increased evidence suggests that mindfulness meditation—a state of actively focusing attention on the present—can ease stress. The beauty of this technique is that there's no 'right' way to do it. Through focusing on the current moment, we can shed anxieties about the past or worries about the future.

Here's how to try mindfulness meditation:

1. Begin by finding a quiet, comfortable place to sit upright.

2. Bring your full attention to your breath—how it goes in and out.

3. If your mind starts to wander, don't judge yourself harshly. Instead, kindly bring your focus back to your breath.

4. Practice for a few minutes initially, gradually increasing up to 20 minutes or more a day.

9.5. Regular Exercise

A host of studies confirm that physical activity can strengthen our ability to endure stress. Physiologically, exercise reduces adrenaline and cortisol levels and stimulates endorphin production—the body's natural mood boosters. Any form of physical activity—a brisk walk, dance, or a game of tennis—can act as a potent stress reliever.

Incorporating exercise into your routine:

1. Make it a goal to do at least 30 minutes of moderate-intensity physical activity most days.

2. Choose activities you enjoy to make it more fun and lasting.

3. If time is an issue, break down your exercise sessions into shorter 10-minute spurts.

9.6. Healthy Eating

While we overlook nutrition under stress, research underscores that what we feed our body can significantly influence how we handle stress. A balanced diet rich in fruits, vegetables, lean proteins, whole grains, and healthy fats can aid in better stress management.

Some nutrition-focused strategies include:

1. Eating balanced meals and snacks evenly spaced throughout the day.

2. Emphasizing whole foods, fruits, and vegetables over processed foods.

3. Keeping yourself well-hydrated.

4. Limiting caffeine and alcohol, which can heighten stress responses.

9.7. Developing Social Networks

Interacting with others, whether friends, family, or larger community groups, can serve as an excellent stress buffer. The sense of belonging, compassion, and understanding you get from healthy social interactions helps enhance your resilience against stressors.

Here's how to foster a supportive network:

1. Make time for face-to-face interaction with loved ones.

2. Seek new friendships and maintain the old ones.

3. Volunteer in your community or a group aligned with your interests.

4. Be open about your feelings to trusted individuals.

Each strategy encapsulates a wealth of scientific insights revolving around the neuroscience of stress. Combining these techniques, tailored to your preference, can help fashion a well-rounded and sustainable stress management regimen. The key, though, is to remain patient and persistent as your brain adapts to these healthier responses. Here lies an opportunity to reclaim control over your stress, thereby promoting an enhanced quality of life and wellbeing.

Remember, a stress-free life may not be possible, but a life where stress is judiciously managed certainly is.

Chapter 10. Nutrition and Activity: Physical Allies Against Stress

Our brain, the ever-buzzing command center, requires certain fuel to perform optimally. With the right nutrition coupled with consistent physical activity, it can better handle stressful situations. Let's elucidate the science behind this phenomenon and provide practical lifestyle changes.

10.1. The Power of Balanced Nutrition

Nutrition plays a pivotal role in the functioning of our brain and body, even more so when coping with stress. When we're under stress, the body ramps up production of the hormone cortisol. High cortisol levels can lead to weight gain, high blood pressure, and lower immunity. A balanced diet can help counter these effects.

Eating nutrient-dense meals nourishes the body and the mind, helping to moderate cortisol levels and regulate other stress-related hormones. A well-balanced diet includes complex carbohydrates, lean proteins, healthy fats, and plenty of fruits and vegetables.

Carbohydrates stimulate the body's production of serotonin, a mood-stabilizing neurotransmitter. Opt for complex carbs such as whole grains, vegetables, and fruits, which are absorbed slowly and lead to a steadier serotonin production.

Proteins rich in the amino acid tryptophan contribute to serotonin production. Lean proteins, like fish, turkey, or beans, are excellent choices.

Healthy fats, like Omega-3 and Omega-6, improve brain function and mood. Sources include fish, flaxseeds, and walnuts.

Avoid high-sugar, high-fat foods despite the short-term comfort they might provide. They can heighten cortisol levels and lead to unhealthy weight gain. Instead, nourish your body with wholesome foods—an investment your body and mind will thank you for.

10.2. Hydrate Your Brain

Don't neglect hydration in the name of nutrition. Dehydration increases the production of cortisol, so maintaining optimal hydration levels is vital. Drinking approximately 2-3 litres a day, depending on your climate and activity levels, can help keep stress and dehydration at bay.

10.3. Supplementation: A Helping Hand

Sometimes, despite our best efforts, our diet might fall short in providing essential nutrients—this is where carefully selected supplements step in. For instance, B vitamins have been found to help reduce stress levels, by aiding the brain in producing mood-regulating hormones. Magnesium can regulate the nervous system and prevent stress-induced calcium build-up. St John's Wort, Omega-3, and probiotics have also been associated with improved mood and resiliency to stress. Consult your healthcare provider before starting any supplementation regimen.

10.4. Physical Activity: A Powerful Tool

Physical activity is another significant piece of the anti-stress puzzle.

Regular exercise is a natural mood-booster, thanks to the production of endorphins—our 'feel good' hormones. It can also improve sleep quality, a factor often impacted by stress.

Starting small, such as a 20-minute daily walk, can lead to improved physical and mental health. Choose an activity you enjoy, be it yoga, swimming, cycling, or dancing, and make it part of your routine. Regular exercise does not just benefit your body; it enhances your brain's resilience to stress.

10.5. Mind-Body Exercises for Stress Relief

Mind-body exercises, like yoga, tai chi, or meditation, can provide major stress relief benefits. These practices furnish a break from stressors and allow for a focus on the present moment—an excellent tool for decompressing the mind. Further, they foster a better awareness of our bodies, making it easier to notice the presence of stress and deal with it effectively.

10.6. Sleep Hygiene for Better Stress Management

Quality sleep is as crucial as nutrition and exercise for managing stress levels. Poor or insufficient sleep can exacerbate stress and cause a vicious cycle of stress and sleeplessness.

Stick to a sleep schedule, create a relaxing bedtime routine, assess your sleep environment, and consider suitable dietary adjustments to promote better sleep. Research has shown that reducing caffeine and alcohol intake, especially closer to bedtime, can contribute to a better night's rest.

In essence, nutrition, hydration, exercise, and sleep are four pillars to combat stress and equip your brain with the tools it needs to thrive. Keep a dedicated focus on these areas—the journey towards better stress management starts with putting these practical lifestyle changes into action.

Remember, every small step taken today will bring you closer to a healthier, stress-resilient life. As always, consult your healthcare provider before making any drastic change to your diet, exercise routine, or supplement intake. After all, every individual's needs and reactions to stress are unique and require personalized care.

Chapter 11. Rewiring the Brain: Adopting a Mindset for Resilience

While the concept of "rewiring" your brain may sound like science fiction, it is a reality backed by potent research in the field of neuroscience. In fact, the plasticity of our brains—that is, our brain's capacity for change—plays a central role in enhancing our resilience to stress, thus helping us to manage and overcome stress more effectively. In this journey, we'll explore how you can adopt a mindset for resilience, enabling you to 'rewire' your brain in the face of stress and adversity.

11.1. Unveiling Neuroplasticity: The Changing Brain

Our brain's ability to change and "wire" itself is known as neuroplasticity. Borrowing from the words "neuron" and "plasticity," it represents our brain's dynamic ability to continuously learn new things, form new connections, and strengthen or weaken existing ones depending on our experiences, behaviors, and environment.

Previously, scientists believed that the brain was sort of "set in stone" after it developed during early childhood. However, our understanding has evolved drastically. We've found that our brains can actually change throughout our entire life—a testament to their profound flexibility.

Up until a few decades ago, it was accepted that each brain cell, or neuron, was hard-wired to perform only a specific function. Any damage to these specialized cells was considered irreversible, leaving lasting, unchangeable impacts.

Modern neuroscience, however, paints a different picture. Now we understand that our brains are much more malleable than we ever imagined. Even when neurons die or are injured, other neurons can adapt and change to take over the functions of the lost cells—an idea referred to as "neural compensation."

This new understanding points to stunning possibilities concerning the human brain's resilience in the face of damage or diseases, as well as the mental fortitude that's possible amidst psychological challenges, like stress.

===The Science behind Stress and Brain Wiring

To understand how stress affects our brains, we must first delve into the world of brain wiring. Every experience we have—positive, neutral, or stressful—triggers a unique pattern of neuronal activity in our brain. To manage these complex experiences, our brains form billions of intricate networks of neurons that communicate through 'synapses.'

When we're stressed, our body releases a hormone called cortisol. This hormone triggers an intricate sequence of events in our brain that influence how we perceive, respond to, and remember the stressful event. Prolonged exposure to stress—and thus sustained high levels of cortisol—can cause neurons to shrink and synapses to weaken, negatively affecting our memory, attention, and decision-making abilities.

11.2. The Role of Mindset in Stress Resilience

Mindset plays a crucial role in our brain's ability to manage stress. Neuroscientist Dr. Alia Crum of Stanford University has conducted groundbreaking research in this area. She's found that people who perceive stress as something negative have a higher risk of health issues. Conversely, those who acknowledge stress as a natural response to external challenges that can be used positively for growth and resilience, fare markedly better, both mentally and physically.

This idea dovetails with psychologist Carol Dweck's notion of a "growth mindset." This perspective frames challenges as opportunities for progress, while a "fixed mindset" perceives them as threats. A shift in perspective from a fixed to a growth mindset can help us realize that stress, while uncomfortable, indicates our engagement with life's challenges and opportunities for growth.

11.3. Transforming Stress: A Resilience Mindset

A 'resilience mindset' doesn't mean that you'd never experience stress; rather, it represents a perspective that empowers you to interpret and respond to stress in more resilient ways.

Let's explore some steps towards cultivating such a mindset:

1. **Awareness**: Start by recognizing your stress response patterns, triggers, and how you typically deal with stress. This self-awareness is the first step towards consciously changing your response to stress.

2. **Reframe Stress**: Instead of viewing stress as an entirely negative event, see it as a part of life's challenges and an opportunity for personal growth and learning.

3. **Practice Mindfulness**: Mindfulness can be a potent tool in fostering a resilience mindset. By bringing non-judgmental awareness to your thoughts, feelings, and the present moment, you can recognize stress patterns and respond to them more effectively.

4. **Cognitive Reappraisal**: This strategy involves changing the way

you interpret stressors. Instead of viewing a challenging situation as a threat, perceive it as an opportunity.

5. **Nurture Positive Relationships**: Social connections play a pivotal role in our stress resilience. Supportive relationships can help us feel understood, validated, and less alone in our stress experiences.

Remember, rewiring your brain isn't a quick fix—it's an ongoing process. Be patient with yourself, start small, and celebrate your progress. By consciously choosing to foster a resilience mindset, you're reinforcing new neural pathways in your brain, training your brain to manage and overcome stress more effectively. The beauty of a resilient mindset is that it's not fixed but grows stronger with practice over time. Embrace the journey, for it's an investment in a lifelong resilience to stress.

www.ingramcontent.com/pod-product-compliance
Lightning Source LLC
Chambersburg PA
CBHW070741260726
48660CB00007B/2930